Color this page to make it your own. Then find things to color throughout the book!

MW01110047

To escape the evil King Herod, an angel told Joseph to flee to Egypt with Jesus and Mary. Years passed, and the king died. Then an angel again came to Joseph in a dream and said, "Get up! It's safe to leave Egypt now. Take Jesus and His mother and go back to Israel."

So Joseph woke up and did just that. The family settled in the town of Nazareth, in the area of Galilee, in the land of Israel. And that's where Jesus grew up.

Every year, Mary and Joseph traveled all the way to the city of Jerusalem to celebrate the Passover Festival. When Jesus was twelve years old, He went with them. After the festival, Mary and Joseph started the long journey back home. They were traveling with a large group of family and friends, and they thought Jesus was with them—but He wasn't!

All through the city, Mary and Joseph searched for Jesus. They looked high and they looked low, but He was nowhere to be found! At last, after three days of searching, they found Him. Jesus was sitting in the temple, listening to the teachers and asking questions.

"Jesus!" Mary said. "Your father and I have been searching everywhere for You! Why have You treated us this way?"

But Jesus said, "Why did you search for Me? Didn't you know I had to be in My Father's house?"

Mary didn't really understand what Jesus' words meant, but she stored them in her heart to think about later. Jesus went back to Nazareth with His parents and obeyed them in all things. He grew taller and wiser, and He pleased both God and people.

Now John, who was the son of Mary's relative Elizabeth, also grew up. He went out into the wilderness to preach about the Savior who was coming. He told people that they should be baptized to show that they were truly sorry for their sins. (That's why he was called John the Baptist.)

Some people asked John if *he* was the Savior. "No!" said John. "I only baptize you with water, but He will baptize you with the Holy Spirit. I'm not even good enough to untie His sandals."

Then, one day, Jesus asked John to baptize Him. But John said, "No! You should baptize me!"

"This is the way it has to be," Jesus told him.

So John baptized Jesus in the Jordan River. As Jesus came up out of the water, the heavens opened up, and the Spirit of God came down on Him like a dove. Then the voice of God spoke from heaven and said, "This is My beloved Son!"

The Holy Spirit came and led Jesus into the wilderness. For forty days and forty nights, Jesus ate nothing at all. After that, He was very hungry! Then the Devil came to tempt Him, saying, "If You're really the Son of God, turn these stones to bread."

But Jesus said, "It is written: Man must not live on bread alone but on every word that comes from God."

Next, the Devil took Jesus to the city of Jerusalem. They stood on the very tiptop of the temple, and the Devil said, "If You're really the Son of God, throw Yourself off this temple. For it is written: His angels will not even let your foot strike against a stone."

But Jesus said, "It is also written: Do not test the Lord your God."

The Devil then took Jesus to the top of a very high mountain and showed Him all the kingdoms of the world and their riches. "I'll give You all these things," the Devil said, "if You'll worship me."

But Jesus said, "Go away, Satan! For it is written: Worship the Lord your God, and serve only Him!"

Then the Devil left Him, and angels came and served Him.

Jesus went back to Galilee and began teaching the people about God. He was filled with the power of the Holy Spirit, and everyone was amazed by His words.

When it was time to choose His disciples, Jesus went up on a mountain by Himself. All night long, He prayed to God. The next morning, Jesus chose twelve men to be His disciples. They were Peter, Andrew, James, John, Philip, Bartholomew, Matthew, Thomas, James the son of Alphaeus, Thaddeus, Simon, and Judas—the one who would betray Him.

Jesus came to earth as a baby and grew up—just like you. He bumped His head and skinned His knees—just like you. And when Jesus was tempted to do wrong, He used God's Word to defeat the Devil! He did for us what we can't do—keep God's commandments perfectly.

Jesus told him, "Go away, Satan! For it is written: Worship the Lord your God, and serve only Him."
—Matthew 4:10

Jesus didn't teach like ordinary teachers; He taught with the power of God! And He didn't teach ordinary lessons. Jesus taught that true righteousness comes from the inside. None of us are righteous on the inside. We are sinners, but when we trust in Jesus and the perfect life *He* lived, God changes us from the inside out.

"I am the way, the truth, and the life.
No one comes to the Father except through Me."
—John 14:6

"But everyone who doesn't obey My words," Jesus warned, "will be like the foolish man who built his house on the sand. The rains poured down, and the waters rose all around. The winds roared and howled and beat against his house—and it came crashing down!"

Jesus taught the people many things that day, and they were amazed by His words.

Then Jesus taught the people about two kinds of builders: "Everyone who obeys My words is like the wise man who built his house on the rock. The rains poured down, and the waters rose all around. The wind roared and howled and beat against his house. But his house did not fall because it was built on the rock.

"And don't worry about what you'll eat or drink or wear," said Jesus. "Just look at the birds: they don't plant food, but God feeds them. And look at the flowers: not even King Solomon was dressed as beautifully as the flowers. And you're worth much more than birds or flowers!

"If you will obey God and put Him first in your life, He will take care of you," Jesus promised.

"Don't worry about getting lots of treasures here on earth," Jesus said. "Those treasures can be stolen by thieves or eaten up by moths or rust. Collect treasures in heaven by doing what God says. Those treasures can *never* be stolen or destroyed!

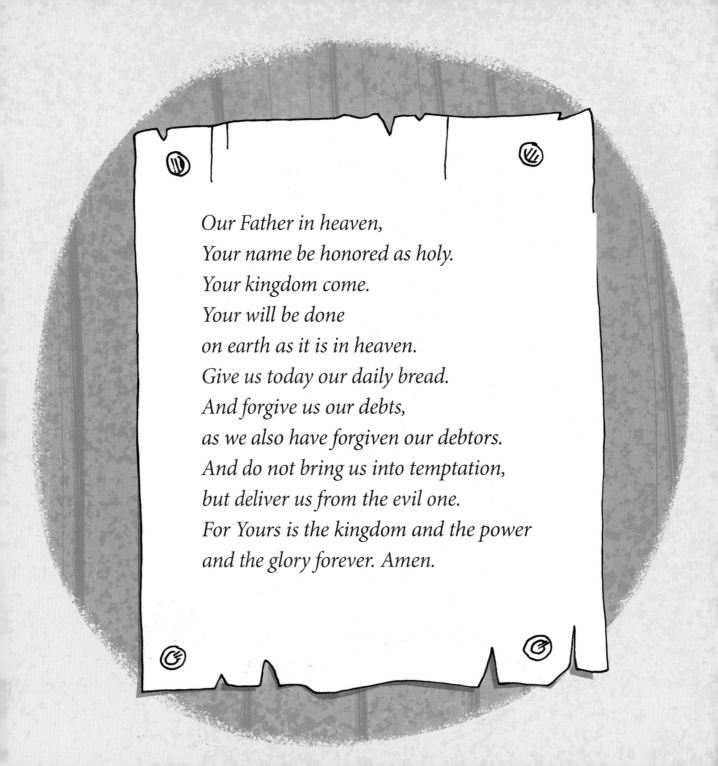

Our Father in heaven,
Your name be honored as holy.
Your kingdom come.
Your will be done
on earth as it is in heaven.
Give us today our daily bread.
And forgive us our debts,
as we also have forgiven our debtors.
And do not bring us into temptation,
but deliver us from the evil one.
For Yours is the kingdom and the power
and the glory forever. Amen.

"And be careful how you pray," Jesus said. "Some people love to pray standing up where everyone can see them. Don't pray just so that others will see you. Go into a quiet room, close the door, and pray in secret. God will hear you, and He'll reward you. And don't just say a lot of words, over and over again. God knows what you need, even before you ask Him! So pray like this:

"When you give to the poor, don't let anyone see you. God will still see you, and He will reward you."

Jesus also taught the people about the right way to give: "You must be careful how you give," He warned. "Don't give to the poor just to show off in front of others. Some people even sound the trumpets when they give, so that everyone will cheer for them. Don't be like them! They already have their reward from the people, so they won't get a reward from God.

"After all, if you only love those who love you back, how are you being a child of God? And if you only talk to those who talk to you, how are you different from anyone else? Anyone can do that! I want you to love your neighbors *and* your enemies too."

"Some people say that you should love your neighbor and hate your enemies," Jesus said. "But I say, love your enemies and pray for those who do wrong to you. That's what the children of God do.

"You are the salt of the earth," Jesus taught, "and the light of the world. No one lights a lamp and then hides it under a basket where no one can see it shine. No! The lamp is put up on a stand so that its light will fill the house. In the same way, the good things that you do should shine in the world like a bright light. They should show everyone the goodness of God in heaven."

Crowds of people gathered to hear Jesus. They had heard about Him and all the miracles He had done, and they wanted to see and hear Him for themselves. When Jesus saw the crowds, He went up on a mountain, sat down, and began to teach them.

He surprised the people by saying the humble and gentle people of the world are blessed by God. Those who are merciful, pure in heart, and poor in spirit are blessed.

But Jesus also warned them that some people would say bad things about them and would even be mean to them because they believed in God. "But you'll be blessed because of that," Jesus said, "and your reward in heaven will be great!"

Color this page to make it your own. Then find things to color throughout the book!